TENANT SCREENING
For The Small Asset Landlord

Pierre Mouchette

Real Property Experts LLC
a Real Estate Knowledge Publication

Copyright © 2021 by Pierre Mouchette

All rights reserved. No part of this publication may be reproduced, distributed, or transmitted in any form or by any means, including photocopying, recording, or other electronic or mechanical methods, without the prior written permission of the publisher, except in the case of brief quotations embodied in critical reviews and specific other noncommercial uses permitted by copyright law.

ISBN 979 - 8411795653 (Paperback Book)

Independently Published

First Edition: February 2022
Real Property Experts LLC
Web Address: https://www.rpe4u.com
Contact: publications@rpe4u.com

Note: This publication comes in various formats, such as Paperbacks and Electronic Books (ebooks). Particular material in the paperback version of this book may not be included in ebooks, and vice versa.

Disclaimer

This Real Property Experts LLC (RPE) publication provides information about the subject matter covered. The author and publisher of this content are not acting as licensed professionals to present covered material. The information and statements made are for educational purposes and are not intended to replace a one-on-one relationship with a qualified attorney, accountant, tax professional, or other licensed professionals. You are exclusively responsible for the use of any content. You hold Real Property Experts LLC, its subsidiaries, and members harmless in any event or claim, demand, or damage, including reasonable attorneys' fees, asserted by any third party, or arising out of your use of, or conduct on, publications and products.

RPE writers provide applicable content and break down complex topics so they are easier to understand. Information given may not apply to your specific situation, and products or services recommended may not be a good fit for your application. While RPE strives to provide accurate, up-to-date content, we cannot guarantee the accuracy and completeness of the information supplied. By using this content, you understand that all material is an expression of opinion and not professional advice.

RPE advises the reader to keep up to date on activities in their locale by consulting with the appropriate licensed professionals for decisions that could affect them.

PREFACE

Your rental property is an investment, and that is not something to be taken lightly, especially when entrusting that investment to someone you do not know. Yes, a certain amount of risk is assumed when you take on the role of LANDLORD, but you can mitigate potential losses by performing your due diligence.

What about damages that this unknown tenant may cause? Will the security deposit cover all or just some of the damage that could potentially happen? What happens when the damage is so severe that the unit cannot be rented out for months? Yes, these are unknown factors of what can occur during a tenancy and why it is crucial that, as a landlord, diligence is complete in pre-and post-screening.

Oops, I almost forgot! As I am sure, you did. Time is valuable and cannot be replaced! What is your time worth?

For comments on this publication, please write to us.
{publications@rpe4u.com}

Pierre Mouchette, author

Contents

Chapter 1 Tenant Qualities .... - 9 -
   WHAT IS TENANT SCREENING? .... - 10 -
      Affordability .... - 10 -
      Qualifying The Tenant .... - 10 -
      Tips For Providing Tenant Reference .... - 11 -
      Tenant Requested Reference .... - 13 -
      Eliminate Most Landlord/Tenant Adversity .... - 14 -

Chapter 2 Equal Opportunity - The Law .... - 15 -
   PROTECTED CLASSES .... - 16 -
      Federal Fair Housing Laws .... - 16 -
      State And Local Fair Housing Laws .... - 16 -
      Age And Children Discrimination .... - 17 -

Chapter 3 Tenant Criteria .... - 18 -
   TENANT CRITERIA .... - 19 -
      Tenant Screening .... - 19 -
      Setting Minimum Requirements .... - 19 -
      Pre-Screening Potential Tenants .... - 19 -
      Pre-Screening Through Advertising .... - 20 -
      Pre-Screening Through Your Phone .... - 20 -
      Pre-Screening In Person .... - 21 -
      During Pre-Screening, Be Aware Of The Following .... - 21 -
   GUIDELINES TO SCREENING PROSPECTIVE TENANTS .... - 23 -
      Have Written Rental Standards That You Use Consistently .... - 23 -
      Measuring Each Prospect On The Same Criteria .... - 23 -
      Use A Solid, Detailed Rental Application .... - 23 -
      Call Previous And Current Landlords .... - 24 -
      Call To Verify Employment .... - 24 -
      Use A Third-Party Screening Service .... - 25 -
      Application Fees .... - 25 -

  Verify Terms..- 26 -

  Always Aim For A Quick Turnaround ....- 26 -

  When You Accept A Tenant, Require Them To Put Down At Least One Month's Rent (Immediately)! ....- 26 -

  Call The New Tenant A Week After Move-In ....- 26 -

 AGGRESSIVE OR LARGE BREED CANINES ....- 27 -

 HOW MUCH SECURITY DEPOSIT? ....- 28 -

  Never Let A Tenant Use The Deposit ....- 28 -

 SCREENING TIPS TO HELP KEEP YOU SAFE ....- 29 -

  Vehicle Check ....- 29 -

  Drive-by Their Current Residence ....- 29 -

  Pay Attention To The Prospects Concerns.................................- 29 -

Chapter 4 DUE DILIGENCE ....- 31 -

 TENANT INCOME AND YOUR DUE DILIGENCE.........................- 32 -

  The Application ....- 34 -

  Supplementary Questions to Ask ....- 34 -

 BACKGROUND AND CREDIT CHECK ....- 36 -

 CONSUMER REPORTS - WHAT YOU NEED TO KNOW ....- 37 -

  Complying With The FCRA..- 37 -

  What Is A Consumer Report?..- 37 -

  Obtaining A Consumer Report ....- 38 -

  What Is An Adverse Action? ....- 38 -

  Taking An Adverse Action ....- 38 -

  Investigative Reports ....- 39 -

  Disposing Of Consumer Reports ....- 39 -

  Other Considerations ....- 39 -

APPENDIX A ....- 41 -

 Commonly Used Words and Phrases ....- 42 -

APPENDIX B ....- 44 -

 Sample Forms ....- 45 -

 Non-bias (Minimum Resident Standard) ....- 46 -

Preapplication and Notification ....- 48 -

Employment Verification ....- 50 -

Landlord Verification ....- 51 -

Personal Guarantor ....- 52 -

    House Rules and Policies ....- 54 -

House Rules and Policies ....- 56 -

The following are general rules that you will be expected to follow: ....- 56 -

    Letter of Acceptance ....- 65 -

    Acceptance Letter with Lease Agreement...- 66 -

    Welcome New Resident ....- 67 -

    Reason for Non-Acceptance ....- 68 -

As a small asset landlord, we want you to be on the upswing of your rental investments. The information presented in this book will help guide you through the tenant screening process.

As an investor specializing in residential housing and managing your holdings, **tenant screening** is one of the most innovative actions you can take towards making your **property management** work as headache-free as possible while protecting **your investments.**

Remember, for an effectively run real estate business. All **landlords/owners** must create a standard process for pre-screening, screening, approving, and rejecting rental applicants. Doing this can minimize the chance of being brought up on various charges, thereby relieving the stress and headaches that often accompany the managing task.

Chapter 1   Tenant Qualities

WHAT IS TENANT SCREENING?

Screening potential tenants is about digging into their backgrounds and discovering who they are. All applications can be easily manipulated and falsified. Screening means **investigating information provided and analyzing and verifying** the information uncovered.

Affordability
The Ability to Afford the Rent Payment - the first and the most valuable quality of a good tenant is their commitment to pay the rent. With no rent payment, you will be compelled to evict and then be confronted with potentially thousands of dollars' worth of legal expenses, lost rent, and damages. To prevent this impasse, most **property owners** require that tenants earn a minimum of three times as much as the monthly rent from their **documentable employment.**

Many tenants believe they can afford more than they really can. So, it is the function of the landlord to set guidelines for their properties. Three times the monthly rent usually is enough, but four is always better.

Qualifying The Tenant
Always look for a tenant with the following qualities:

- **Willingness to pay on time** - some property owners look at late rent as merely a benefit (with the late fee being a financial bonus to them), but a late-paying tenant is more likely to stop paying altogether. When the rent does not come in, the stress involved is not a pleasant experience that can be avoided by renting to tenants who have a solid history of paying on time.

- **The long-term outlook for job stability** - while a tenant may pay the rent and pay it on time now, their ability to do so in the future is often determined by their employment situation. If they change jobs frequently or have long periods of unemployment, you may find long periods of missed rent.

- **Cleanliness and housekeeping skills** - no tenant stays forever, and when they leave, you want the property returned in good condition. The tenant's day-to-day living should be clean and orderly. They need to take good care of the property you entrusted with them.

- **How much stress will they cause you** - some tenants are high maintenance and continually demand time and attention. If you are not having difficulty finding quality tenants, these types will only cause problems.

- **Tenant must have good references** - the references you receive from past landlords indicate how a tenant will act for you. An inadequate assessment from a past landlord is a red flag for most landlords.

- **No evictions** - a tenant who faced eviction in the past ten years is an unlikely subject for a rental. With the realization that people may change, the question is, **'Is It Worth the Risk?'**

- **Clean background** - if a tenant has a criminal activity background, **'Is It Worth the Risk to Rent to Them?'** Again, people change, but **'Are You Willing to Take the Risk?'**

Tips For Providing Tenant Reference

If you receive a request from a former tenant asking for a reference to their future landlord, you should look at this as an opportunity to help the prospective landlord. After all, landlords must stick together! Just be honest in describing your experiences with a previous tenant, good or bad, without embellishment.

Use the following in providing tenant references:

- **Be honest, above all, tell the truth** - if you lie about a tenant, it could come back to haunt you. Sometimes, a landlord with a bad tenant could be tempted to say anything to a future landlord to help ensure they vacate their property. *The prospective landlord can sue you for misrepresentation if you provide false information.*

- **Be specific, not emotional** - there is no reason to have one blanket description that is not useful. Make it personalized, with a detailed description of your experience with the tenant, and leave emotions out of it. Stick to the facts!

- **Discuss stability** - mention the length of time they lived in your unit and whether they paid rent on time every month. If there were any issues with the rent or utility payments, the new landlord needs to know.

- **Discuss cleanliness** - describe the tenant's level of cleanliness. Did you have pest problems caused by the tenant? Did they trash the carpets or stain the floors?

- **Be accountable** - assume the future tenant will read your letter or listen to your phone conversation. Do not say anything you would not want to be published on the front page. Be able to support any claim you make with proper documentation or evidence.

Tenant Requested Reference
Sample 1-1

LANDLORD REFERRAL for PREVIOUS TENANT(s)

Name:					
Tenant Address:					
City:		State:		Zip Code:	

The above tenant(s) has/have stated that they had a residency at your rental located at:

_____

Please verify the following information. We have included a self-addressed stamped envelope for your convenience. Thank you so much, and we appreciate your cooperation.

Length of Tenancy From:				To:	
Did Tenant	Pay Rent on Time:	☐ Yes	☐ No	(every month)	
	Pay Utilities on Time:	☐ Yes	☐ No		
	Damage the Premises:	☐ Yes	☐ No		
	Keep the Unit Clean:	☐ Yes	☐ No		
	Create Any Type of Infestation:	☐ Yes	☐ No		

Was there any damage other than normal wear and tear?

Comments:

If You Would Like to Expand on Your Comments, Please Feel Free to Do So.

Eliminate Most Landlord/Tenant Adversity

The landlord/tenant relationship has the potential to be adversarial. Adversity is stressful and not good business practice. So, try to avoid trouble. Use the following techniques to support your efforts:

- **Set the tone upfront** - be professional, polite, and respectful towards your potential tenants.

- **Screen your tenants** - not only with credit and background checks but also listen to and observe how they act.

- **If you decide to rent to an applicant** - explain terms and house rules. Take the time to review the documents with your tenants', line by line. Yes, read the lease and all documents to your tenants, so they hear expectations and what will not be tolerated.

- **Respond to repair requests** - and other tenant issues quickly and professionally, even if it is just a text message. It lets the tenant know they are understood, which in itself can go a long way to reducing adversity. Unresponsiveness by the landlord is perhaps the number one complaint.

- **Know when to say when** - let your tenants know that you do not do drama and expect them to act like adults and settle problems like adults. Sometimes you just need to say no, and not get involved.

Chapter 2   Equal Opportunity - The Law

PROTECTED CLASSES

Discriminating against anyone in a protected class is not only morally wrong but illegal. The following will help to remind you of the law.

Federal Fair Housing Laws
The following has been taken from the **U.S. Department of Housing and Urban Development's Fair Housing Website,** which says:

In the Sale and Rental of Housing - no one can take any of the following measures based on race, color, national origin, religion, sex, familial status, or handicap:

- refuse to rent or sell housing
- refuse to negotiate for housing
- deny a home
- deny anyone access to or membership in a facility or service (such as a multiple listing service) related to housing sale or rental
- falsely deny that housing is available for inspection, sale, or rental
- for profit, persuade owners to sell or rent (blockbusting)
- make housing unavailable
- provide different housing services or facilities
- set different contractual terms, conditions, or privileges for the sale or rental of a dwelling

While you must not discriminate against these classes, it is also crucial that you do not even ask questions about specific matters. Do not ask their race, how many kids they have (you can ask how many people will be living there), or if they have a spouse.

The same applies to advertising: **DO NOT advertise "no kids," "great Hispanic neighborhood," or "home great for families."** It is against federal law!

State And Local Fair Housing Laws
Additionally to **Federal Fair Housing Laws,** your state may also have **'landlord-tenant laws'** that comply with fair housing, which might include:

- age
- gender identity
- marital status
- participation in the Section 8 Program or other subsidy programs
- sexual orientation

Be sure to verify your state and local laws to ensure compliance. A simple computer search for **'your state'** and **'fair housing'** will give you the answers you need.

Age And Children Discrimination

As previously mentioned, **Federal Fair Housing laws** prevent discrimination against family status, and it is illegal to prohibit children. Nevertheless, there is an exception to the rule, which states that specific properties may be designated as a **'55+ Community.'**

According to HUD - to qualify for an exemption, the community must satisfy each of the following constraints:

- At a minimum, 80-percent of inhabited units have to be occupied by at least one person 55 years of age or older.

- The owners and management of the housing facility/community must publish and adhere to policies and procedures which demonstrate its intent to provide housing for persons 55 years or older.

- The facility/community must comply with the Secretary's rules to verify occupancy through reliable surveys and affidavits.

Chapter 3   Tenant Criteria

TENANT CRITERIA

Tenant criteria are intended to help you sift through all the information about the **tenant applicants** to find who most closely fits your **tenants' criteria.** No tenant is going to be 100-percent perfect! So, deciding how close you come to **"perfection"** depends on your desired involvement and the **property offerings.**

Tenant Screening

A crucial smart move and a most intelligent step that you can take towards making your property management experience headache-free, in addition to protecting your investment, are:

- Create consistent pre-screening procedures for a well-run real estate business (screening, approving, and rejecting rental applicants).

- Know protected classes and why discrimination is illegal when selecting the best tenants.

- Seek qualities that usually indicate top-notch tenants and be aware of indicators that an applicant might cause future problems.

Setting Minimum Requirements

The most crucial step in screening prospective tenants and finding the most qualified applicant is creating a minimum property requirement list. These standards should be conveyed on the telephone, placed on the application, put in your advertisement, and stated in person to eliminate those who will not qualify.

Pre-Screening Potential Tenants

Screening does not begin with a background check or an application. It starts with the initial contact, also known as **'pre-screening.'** Screening takes a considerable amount of time, and you do not want to **waste your time** on every person who states an interest in your rental. Therefore, pre-screening is essential!

Pre-Screening Through Advertising

Your pre-screening efforts begin with your advertisement. No matter how you advertise, the information provided can help to weed out **time-wasters.** For example:

- In placing a general location or a nearby landmark, you can eliminate those looking for a different area.

- Including the rental amount helps keep those who cannot afford that price range from calling.

- Always state if you accept pets or not.

- State if the building is smoke-free or not.

Pre-Screening Through Your Phone

Carefully listening to the initial call will give you a lot of information about an individual. If the prospective tenant should ask about the property, be sure that you have a checklist prepared so that:

- Everyone receives the same information.

- You cannot be charged with discrimination over the phone.

- You inform them about up-front fees, deposits, first-month rent, etc.

- In the conversation, always include your minimum requirements, such as the minimum income requirement of $_____ per month. And that you do a complete background and criminal check to make sure that you only rent to qualified people.

- A time that they can view the unit.

As a landlord performing the above, it is a win situation. Doing this is what makes the pre-screening process so important. It enables you to save time, avoid nuisances and project a good image.

Pre-Screening In Person

The next step is to meet with prospective tenants and show them the property. It is also an excellent opportunity to screen the applicant before submitting any paperwork. Always restate your minimum requirements, and to reinforce your statement (just in case they did not understand), you should have a pre-application with your standards on it for them to review.

Now and then, a prospective tenant may ask if you could work with them for various reasons (not enough money; credit; or some other reasons since they do not meet your criteria).

- Should you need time to think about it, say that you will have to check with (your partner or any other authority), and you will let them know.

- If you know that they will not qualify, let them know why, but still allow them the opportunity to apply.

- If they do not meet your **written** criteria, you can always inform them of that fact if they ask you to work with them. *Remember, this criterion applies to everyone, and you cannot discriminate!*

During Pre-Screening, Be Aware Of The Following

- **The storyteller** - be careful because they always explain in detail before answering a question. *Even the most straightforward question that should require only a yes or no answer comes with a longwinded story.*

- **They cannot decide** - they have never decided on their own since someone has always done it for them. These individuals often have no clue how to live independently or manage their lives. *They could be problematic during the tenancy.*

- **The deadbeat** - beware, this person is a user, and usually, they are not willing to work or behave responsibly. *This person typically does not pay debts or accept responsibilities.*

- **The perfectionist** - these individuals will drive you crazy since nothing is good enough for them. *In the commercial that shows the tenant calling in the middle of the night, these individuals fit the profile. They will constantly harass you with phone calls about this little thing or that little thing!*

- **The complainer** - this individual complains about their last landlord, the dwelling unit, the other tenants, and more.

- **The all-cash tenant** - looks good on the surface, but what is the background behind this unusual gesture? *Yes, there could be many legitimate reasons, but again it is not normal.*

GUIDELINES TO SCREENING PROSPECTIVE TENANTS

Screening prospects is probably one of the most important topics for **Small Asset Landlords** who self-manage their portfolios. Screening tenants and choosing the most qualified tenants is crucial to the long-term success of a real estate investment portfolio.

Have Written Rental Standards That You Use Consistently
The most effective way to stay out of trouble and keep out of court on discrimination charges. This standard must cover the following topics that every prospective tenant is assessed against (i.e., income, credit history, rent history, application, co-signer, etc.).

Measuring Each Prospect On The Same Criteria
This will make your decision-making more objective. You will become more objective due to having a consistent scoring method based on written rental standards. The applicant can only score into three groups (deny, accept, and above benchmarks).

Use A Solid, Detailed Rental Application
Include the following in your application for all applicants:

- Permission to contact current and previous landlords.

- Always obtain a copy of the following:
  Driver's license (DL) or state-issued picture I.D. Requesting the DL will allow you to verify the address and see if it matches the application documents. It indicates when the DL was issued and confirms the date of birth. It also lets you pair up an applicant with online social networking sites (Facebook, LinkedIn, and Twitter) to learn more about the applicant if necessary. The photo will help you make sure you have the right person.

- Voided personal check (to verify bank).

- Two weeks of the most up-to-date pay stubs of each income source listed.

- If the prospective tenant is self-employed, you should ask for the most current Schedule C tax return and current income proof.

- Child maintenance, alimony, pension check, or other sources of income.

- Proof of auto insurance.

- If you accept pets, get a copy of their picture.

Call Previous And Current Landlords

Prior landlords are MUCH more important than the current landlord. The reason is that the current landlords might be telling you what you want to hear just to get rid of them!

Call To Verify Employment

Sometimes it is challenging to get through to employers. The following are sample questions to use when speaking with employers:

- Is this person employed at your company?

- How long has your company employed them?

- Can you confirm the income they have listed?

- What are the expectations for future employment?

Always ask for their name when thanking them!

When the applicant does not have a previous or current landlord, request three references.

The following are sample questions:

- How do you know this person?

- Tell me about your interaction with them!

- Can you share a few words to describe them!

- Were they reliable and trustworthy?

- If a neighbor, have been they good neighbors? Quiet? Considerate of their neighbors? Did they keep their property clean?

Use A Third-Party Screening Service

An important step is to use one of the screening services available to landlords. Ensure that you receive a credit score, criminal background (local, county, state, and national level), sex offender information, eviction history, collections, and public records with any reporting service used.

Application Fees

Take application fees for the qualifying applicants, not as a profit generator but to cover the costs incurred in obtaining screening reports. Even more important is that the fees serve as a level of commitment to the property. It makes applicants think before they apply, and if they pay the application fee and back out, at least your costs are covered.

Do not treat the application fees as a revenue stream because you do not want to have a reputation for taking application fees and not accepting the applicants.

Note: a good practice might be to refund applicants' fees if they are not selected and retain them if they lie on their application or choose to back out.

Always require an application fee (cash or money order; NEVER a check).
Be sure the **'tour guide'** tells the prospective tenants that there are no guarantees their application will be accepted, and application fees are **NON-REFUNDABLE.**

Verify Terms

The prospective tenant must be aware of your terms. Yes, the lease states the words, but people do not always read leases meanwhile missing something. Be proactive and send out an email called **'Pre-Rental Acceptance Email.'** This email summarizes the terms included, such as rent, deposit, duration, who pays what utilities, parking, etc.

In this email, you should attach the condo association rules and regulations (if a condo) and your tenant expectation **GUIDE**. Always have the applicants reply to the email that they agree with the terms and the attachments. Even though all terms are in the lease, this email will help to prevent future issues.

Always Aim For A Quick Turnaround

Moving is stressful. When a tenant applies, be sure you inform them of your expectations and how much time your underwriting will take. Attempt to get your questions back to the tenant within the first 24 hours and demand a quick turnaround from them as well.

When You Accept A Tenant, Require Them To Put Down At Least One Month's Rent (Immediately)!

This is a HUGE point! Do not stop marketing until you get a security deposit from the prospective tenant. Remember, without any skin in the game, potential tenants will have no problem walking from the unit and finding somewhere else to live. ***Do not stop marketing until you have money in your hand!***

Call The New Tenant A Week After Move-In

This is a simple step that most landlords forget to do. It is essential to check in with the tenant and make sure they know you are there for them and happy to make their tenancy as comfortable as possible. Also, you can use this follow-up to ensure they have transferred the utilities into their name!

AGGRESSIVE OR LARGE BREED CANINES

Tenants with Pit Bulls, Rottweilers, Chows, Akitas, and any cross breed with a wolf or any of the above mixes could be problems. Chances are that your insurance company does not allow these types or breeds either.

Chihuahuas bite more people than most breeds. But, they do not kill them. The dog's nature is in the species, and all an owner can do is depress or enhance it.

If your tenant has an aggressive breed dog, avoid them at all costs.

The preceding is presented as a guide, not a must for qualification or disqualification. Set up a standard in written format to guide your actions to be fair across the board.

HOW MUCH SECURITY DEPOSIT?

A security deposit is always worth more than prepaid rent. Prepaid rent is used by and for the tenant; the security deposit is 100-percent used by the landlord to make them **whole** again. The landlord should always keep the security deposit until the tenant has vacated and a complete inspection has been made to assess damages. Then, the landlord must return the deposit less any deductions, with an included itemized list stating what deductions were made.

Note: some states dictate when the security deposit will be returned.

The security amount is determined by:

- The state (some states allow a maximum of one month's rent for a security deposit).

- If allowed, always try to secure two months' rent.

If the applicant states that they do not have enough for the full deposit, you should consider this a red flag!

- If the tenant does not have emergency funds, and that is what they tell you when they do not have a full deposit, you need to run away. Why? They should be getting a full deposit back from their previous landlord, which can be used to replace the emergency funds that they give you.

- Deposits paid after move-in never happen! Always collect your full deposit before any keys are turned over.

Never Let A Tenant Use The Deposit
Some tenants like to use the deposit for the last month's rent. This tenant expects you to trust them to return the rental without any damages and as clean as they received it.

SCREENING TIPS TO HELP KEEP YOU SAFE

Vehicle Check

Consistently meet and greet prospective tenants at the curb when they pull up for a showing. Look at their vehicle and consider:

- If it purrs like a kitten and is washed and waxed, you know that they can either afford it or are obsessed with it. Check their financials to determine which applies.

- If the outside is beat up, that could mean they are not incredibly responsible with their possessions, but it might also mean that they got into an accident and cannot afford the bodywork.

- If the inside is damaged, you do not want these people on your property. The interior of a car is the second-best thing you can see to the inside of their current home.

Drive-by Their Current Residence

As part of the process, pop into their current residence. If necessary, bring them some information that you need to give them. Do not expect to or ask to be invited in.

- Listen for indicators of pets or anything else that might make you consider their tenancy.

- Get whatever kind of peek you can inside and pay attention to smell and condition. Are they hoarders?

- You may be able to tell right away if someone is a smoker or has mold inside their living space and a whole host of other potential turn-offs just by smelling their home.

Pay Attention To The Prospects Concerns

A prospective tenant's concerns can tell you a lot about them.

- If they are in a huge hurry to move and not because of a job, it is most likely due to an impending eviction. Get the full story!

- If they are concerned that the house is not worth the rent you are asking for, it is seldom because of the house. They are worried about paying the rent. Also, some people like to complain, and do you want a tenant who likes to complain?

- If they have many complaints about their current landlord, Google them. It may be they legitimately had a horrible landlord, or it might be that they are awful tenants and do not realize it.

- If they are focused on paying online or in cash, it might be because they are receiving their money from an uncomfortable source.

- If they are concerned about the neighbors' tolerance for crowds or noise, they might be looking for a party pad. That is not necessarily a deal-breaker, but it is something to consider carefully.

- If they are concerned about the neighbors being snoopy, it is an almost surefire indication that they plan to do something they do not want to be discovered.

There is a lot that a reliable tenant screening company can do, but there is also a lot that they cannot. Get personally involved and pay attention. Your senses and intuition are your best friends.

Chapter 4　　DUE DILIGENCE

TENANT INCOME AND YOUR DUE DILIGENCE

As a **Small Asset Landlord,** part of what you do is take applications from prospective tenants. This process, also known as due diligence, gives insight into the prospective tenant's qualifications to obtain tenancy, especially regarding their ability to pay the rent and maintain the property.

The following forms indicate income or compensation received for the previous year.

- **Federal income tax return (IRS 1040)** - is the most comprehensive way of verifying income. It is a complete document, whereas the potential tenant might not remember all sources of revenue.

- **Employee income statement (Form W-2)** - a statement sent from an employer to its workers at the end of the tax year. It contains information about wages earned and taxes withheld from their paychecks.

- **Self-employed earnings (Form 1099-MISC)** - are used to report various types of reportable income (compensation), such as amounts paid to an independent contractor for services rendered.

Current compensation is indicated on a payroll stub. This will show the current status and may display raises or promotions. The Payroll Check Stub must comply with the **Fair Labor Standards Act (FLSA)**, which regulates issues like payroll record-keeping for employers, and state-based requirements such as:

- Employer Name, Address, and Telephone Number.
- Employee Name and Address.
- Social Security Number (masked).
- Date Issued.
- Pay Period.
- Net Pay.
- Pay and Withholding.

Note: it is crucial to obtain the W-2 or 1099-MISC and a compliant pay stub. Receiving the filed copy of IRS 1040 is like icing on the cake.

A non-compliant payroll stub - is a paid receipt that the applicant receives every week.

- Pro: Simple to find and is current.
- Con: You must verify the document with the employer.

Letter from Applicant's Employer - this is typically easy to get for tenants, and if the employer references the tenant's work ethic, you have increased your comfort level.

- Pro: The employer can give qualitative feedback on the potential tenant. *The letter must be on company stationery.*
- Con: Can be easily forged. *Call and thank the person who wrote the letter to verify they wrote it.*

Social Security Statement (SSA-1099) - a tax form mailed annually in January to individuals who receive Social Security benefits. It indicates the total amount of benefits received from Social Security in the previous year.

Annuity Statement - this is a contract between a person and an insurance company where they are promised a steady cash flow stream in exchange for a lump sum of cash.

- Pro: Consistent, verifiable income.
- Con: This income usually has an end date. *You must verify the statement's expiration date.*

Pension Distribution Statement (1099-MISC) - Self Employed Earnings

- Pro: A consistent source of income.
- Con: The distribution amount can change.

Workman's Compensation Letter - is a letter issued by an insurance company or a court awarding compensation.

- Pro: Easy to verify.
- Con: Verify the term of payment.

Court Ordered Awards Letter - a document produced by the court showing a mandated payment.

- Pro: Court-mandated.
- Con: The court order can be appealed.

Interest and Dividend Income - can be found on the tax return or a brokerage statement. On the tax return, there will be a 1099-INT and a 1099-DIV.

- Pro: Reliable income source.
- Con: Usually a small amount.

The Application

This is a window into your tenant's life. It is crucial that you ask the right questions and not ask the wrong ones. The following is a list of must-haves to incorporate on your tenancy application:

- Name, address, phone number, driver's license number
- Social security number and date of birth
- Current and past landlords with contact info
- Employer and job details with contact info
- Have they ever had an eviction filed upon them or broken a lease
- Release of information signature

Such issues are essential for knowing the potential tenant's history.

Supplementary Questions to Ask

The following are additional questions you may want to ask a prospective tenant:

- Requested move-in day?
- How many animals do you have, and what types?
- What could interrupt your ability to pay rent?
- Do you have sufficient cash to pay the first month's rent and security deposit?

- Do you have a checking account and savings account?
- How many people will be living in the dwelling?
- Emergency contacts?
- How is your credit, explain?
- How did you hear about this listing?

The application must be complete. If it is not, send it back immediately, and ask for it to be finished. If they forgot one small section, you could make a phone call to obtain the missing information. But you should train your tenant to follow your policies, and it begins here.

BACKGROUND AND CREDIT CHECK

What distinguishes a Background Check from a Credit Check?

- A background check looks at the tenant's criminal and eviction history and looks for fraud or deception.
- A credit check looks at the renter's ability to pay their bills and obligations responsibly.

Use a screening service such as **SmartMove,** which is offered by TransUnion. Some of the benefits provided are:

- No site inspection is needed.
- Includes **BOTH** criminal and credit backgrounds.
- The Tenant applies and pays online.
- The information is sent to both the applicant and the landlord.
- The report is transmitted immediately.

CONSUMER REPORTS - WHAT YOU NEED TO KNOW

In using consumer reports to make tenant decisions, the **Fair Credit Reporting Act** requires you to take essential compliance steps. Keep your actions within the law if you look at housing applicants or decide whether to renew a current tenant's lease.

Tenant background checks can include various information, such as rental and eviction history, credit, and criminal records. They are also known as **consumer reports.** When using consumer reports to make tenant decisions, you must comply with the **Fair Credit Reporting Act (FCRA).**

Note: The Federal Trade Commission (FTC) enforces the FCRA.

Complying With The FCRA
You must take specific steps before getting a consumer report and after taking adverse action based on information in the statement.

What Is A Consumer Report?
A consumer report may contain information about a person's credit characteristics, rental history, or criminal history. These reports are prepared by a CRA, a business that assembles such reports for other companies and remains covered under the FCRA. Instances comprise:

- Credit reports from a credit bureau, such as Trans Union, Experian, Equifax, or affiliate.

- Report from a tenant screening service, describing the applicant's rental history based on previous landlord information or housing court records.

- A report from a tenant screening service describes the applicant's rental history that includes a credit report the service received from a credit bureau.

- Report from a reference verification service that contacts previous landlords or other parties listed on the rental application on behalf of the property owner.

- Report by a background check company about an applicant or tenant's criminal history.

Obtaining A Consumer Report

You should only acquire a consumer report if you have a lawful purpose. Landlords can obtain consumer reports on applicants and tenants that apply for rental housing or renew a lease. You must obtain written permission from applicants or tenants to show that you have a permissible purpose.

You must certify to the company that you are getting the consumer report that you will only use the information for housing purposes. You cannot use the consumer report for other purposes.

It is also good to review other applicable federal and state laws related to consumer reports. For example, a blanket policy of denying rent to everyone with a criminal record can infringe on the Fair Housing Act.

What Is An Adverse Action?

Any action by a landlord unfavorable to a rental applicant or the tenant's interests. Examples of adverse actions taken include:

- needing a larger deposit than might be required for another applicant
- raising the rent to a higher amount than for another applicant
- requiring a co-signer on the lease
- requiring a deposit that would not be required for another applicant
- you deny the application

Taking An Adverse Action

If you decline an applicant, increase the rent or deposit, require a co-signer, or take other adverse actions based wholly or partly on information in a consumer report. In that case, you must give the applicant or tenant a notice of that fact, verbally, in writing, or electronically.

An adverse action notice informs people about their rights to see reported information and correct inaccurate information. The notice must include:

- The consumer reporting company's name, address, and phone number that supplied the report.

- The company that provided the report did not decide to take adverse action and cannot give specific reasons.

- A notice of the individual's right to dispute the accuracy or completeness of any information the consumer reporting company furnished and receive a free report from the company if requested, within 60 days.

The adverse action notice is mandatory even if the information in the consumer report was not the primary reason for the decision. The applicant or tenant must be notified even if the report's information played only a small part in the overall conclusion.

Although oral adverse action notices are allowed, written notices provide proof of FCRA compliance.

Investigative Reports

Based on personal interviews, landlords who use **Investigative Reports** concerning a person's character, general reputation, personal characteristics, and lifestyle have additional obligations under the FCRA. These obligations include giving **written notice** that the person investigated has the right to request additional disclosures and a summary of the report's scope and substance. (15 U.S.C. section 1681d(a), (b)).

Disposing Of Consumer Reports

After using consumer reports, you must securely dispose of the report and any information you gathered from it, which could include burning, pulverizing, or shredding paper-based documents and disposing of electronic material so that it cannot be read or reconstructed.

Other Considerations

If reporting information, such as late rent payments or evictions, to a company that compiles background information, you have legal obligations under the FCRA's Furnisher Rule. Your responsibilities include:

TENANT SCREENING - For The Small Asset Landlord

- Furnishing information that is accurate and complete.
- Investigating consumer disputes concerning the accuracy of the information you provide.

APPENDIX A

Commonly Used Words and Phrases

Arbitration - to use a neutral third party to resolve a dispute instead of the court.

Agreement - an exchange of promises, a mutual understanding or arrangement, a contract. All agreements must be in writing and acknowledged by all parties.

Consumer Report - a comprehensive report which provides personally identifiable information relating to credit, character, and lifestyle.

Consumer Reporting Agency - an entity that collects and disseminates information about consumers for credit evaluation.

Discrimination - denying a person housing or stating that accommodations are not available because of the individual's race, color, religion, sex, sexual orientation, national origin, ancestry, age, disability, marital or familial status. Treating people differently could be considered discrimination.

Eviction - court proceeding for removing a tenant from a rental when the tenant violates the rental agreement or does not comply with a notice ending the tenancy.

Executed Contract - contracts that are signed by all parties. Sometimes referred to as signed-in counterpart.

Fees - money collected from tenants that are not refundable at the end of the tenancy (applicant screening, pets, cleaning, etc.).

Guests - a person who does not have a tenant's rights but stays in/on the premises for a set period.

Housing Assistance Program (HAP) - temporary (2+ years) housing subsidiary with private landlords: for tenancy in singles, duplexes, multi-family, and apartment buildings. Participants must move into a more permanent housing subsidy after 2-years, such as the **Housing Choice Voucher Program.**

Housing Choice Voucher (HCV) - the housing choice voucher program is the federal government's program to help low-income families, the elderly, and the disabled to afford decent, safe, and sanitary housing in the private market. Housing assistance is arranged on behalf of a family or an individual. Program participants can find accommodations, including single-family homes, townhouses, and apartments. The participant is free to choose any housing that meets the program's requirements, and it is not restricted to subsidized housing.

Housing Choice Vouchers are managed by public housing agencies (PHAs). These local PHAs receive federal funds from the U.S. Department of Housing and Urban Development (HUD) to administer the voucher program.

Inspection Checklist - a written checklist or statement describing the condition and cleanliness of the premises and its furnishings.

Lessee - the tenant.

Lessor - the property owner.

Rental Criteria - a set of written standards that an applicant must meet to qualify for tenancy. These criteria must be applied to rental selections consistently and fairly to avoid fair housing issues.

Section 8 - a federally funded government program. The U.S. Department of Housing and Urban Development (HUD) regulates the Section 8 program, while the Housing Authority administers the program at the local level. The program is designed to assist very low-income families, the elderly, and the disabled to rent decent, safe, and sanitary housing. A housing subsidiary is paid directly to the landlord on behalf of a participating family.

Tenant - one or more persons who occupy the real estate for a fixed period.

Tenant Screening - a process property owners use to evaluate prospective tenants to ascertain if the applicant will fulfill the rental agreement terms. This process culminates in deciding whether to approve the applicant, approve conditionally (requiring a co-signer), or deny tenancy.

APPENDIX B

TENANT SCREENING - For The Small Asset Landlord

Sample Forms

For the reader's convenience, we have provided sample forms that can be used as a starting point to design your forms in conjunction with your legal professional. All documents used **MUST comply with Federal, State, and local laws.**

SAMPLE	DESCRIPTION
B-1	Minimum Criteria and Checklist for Resident Selection
B-2	Preapplication and Notification
B-3	Employment Verification
B-4	Landlord Verification
B-5	Personal Guarantee
B-6	House Rules and Policies
B-7	Letter of Acceptance
B-8	Acceptance Letter with Lease Agreement
B-9	Welcome New Resident
B-10	Reason for Non-Acceptance

TENANT SCREENING - For The Small Asset Landlord

Non-bias (Minimum Resident Standard)
MINIMUM CRITERIA and CHECKLIST FOR RESIDENT SELECTION

Automatic Disqualification

	The apartment applied for is in a nonsmoking building, and the applicant(s) smoke.
	The building is a non-pet building, and the applicant has a pet(s).
	Incomplete application.
	The applicant lied on the application.
	Eviction for nonpayment or cause.
	Case for property damage, disturbances, nuisance, foreclosure, or other cause.
	Four (4) or more thirty-day delinquencies, three (3) or more sixty-day delinquencies, any combination of four (4) thirty-day or sixty-day delinquencies.
	One (1) ninety-day or greater delinquency, charge-off, collection, skip, or civil suit.
	Any repossession, tax lien, or bankruptcy.

Give a score of one point (or more when applicable) for each of the following criteria. Add up the total points to see if the applicant reaches the minimum acceptable score.

Financial Criteria	
	Minimum score on the credit report of 650. (Add 1 point for each additional 10 points over 650).
	Sufficient income (Monthly income is three times the rent amount).
	Sufficient income (Monthly income is more than four times the rent amount).
	Verifiable source of income of employment.
	The same source of income for a minimum of one year. (Two years = two points; three years = three points, etc., up to a maximum of five points.) Must provide W-2 forms for proof of income.
	Able to pay full deposit and rent requested.
	Currently paying a comparable amount of rent.
	No negative remarks on the credit report.
	No delinquent payments in the past six months are indicated on the credit report.
	No excessive financial obligations (more than 50 percent of income).
	Has a checking account.
	Has a savings account.
	Able to provide three credit references.
	No late notices from the current landlord.
	No prior evictions.
	Able to provide a co-signer (two points if co-signer owns real estate).

_____ Total (maximum forty points this section).

TENANT SCREENING - For The Small Asset Landlord

	Rental Stability Criteria
	Resided at current address minimum of one year. (Two years = two points, three years = three points, etc., up to a maximum of five points). Must have been responsible for rent payment.
	No health or safety violations are present upon inspection of the current residence.
	No security deposit was withheld because of property upkeep at the current residence.
	There are no notices from the current landlord regarding a rental agreement violation.
	No neighborhood complaints of residents, pets, or police reports disturbing the peace.
	No pets.
	Good report from the landlord before the current landlord.
	No criminal history.

____ **Total** (maximum fifteen points this section).

	Additional Criteria
	Move-in date within an acceptable time.
	Personal appearance and automobile appearance are neat and clean.
	Will have rent payments electronically paid monthly (add ten points).

____ **Total** (maximum fifteen points this section).

____ **Total criteria points**

Applicant's Total Score			
Date of application:		Date verified:	
Above criteria verified by:		Applicant notified	☐ Acceptance ☐ Denial
Action taken:		By what method:	
Date applicant notified:			
Any other action required:			

For compliance with applicable law, please follow the above minimum standard for tenant selection. The applicant who scores highest over the minimum should be selected to conform to this nonbiased form.

All applicants who do not score above the minimum criteria are ineligible. An adverse letter is required to comply with Fair Credit Reporting Act.

TENANT SCREENING - For The Small Asset Landlord

Preapplication and Notification

Dear Applicant,

We are proud of our rental homes and actively seek only qualified tenants to reside in them. We screen our applicants carefully, and we thoroughly verify all the information provided to us on a rental application. We run a credit report on every applicant, a criminal background check, employment verification, and we check prior rent history.

The screening and verification procedure is used for every applicant the same way, fairly, consistently, and in compliance with Fair Housing Regulations. The applicant who passes the screening criteria is offered a rent when available. Conversely, an applicant who does not satisfy the screening criteria is not accepted as a resident.

By applying for one of our rentals, you acknowledge that all requested information will be completed and give us consent to verify your input. If not complete, the application cannot be processed. We will do everything to process your request quickly (generally within 72 hours). If you have not heard back from us by then, please contact us.

Thank you so much for completing the application for one of our rentals. And, we hope you will become a long-term resident with us. Please read and sign below acknowledging acceptance of the terms of your application.

1. I have double-checked the information provided on the rental application and agree that it is accurate and complete.

2. I understand that an annual update of this application may be requested. I agree to provide updated information and notification to the management of any changes (i.e., employment, phone number, bank, car, emergency contact.).

3. My credit report/history is good. If not, I have attached a separate page to explain my credit problems.

4. I understand and agree that this application is subject to approval based on the information on my application. If any of the information I have given turns out to be FALSE, my application will be denied.

5. I understand and agree that this application is NOT a lease or rental agreement, and should it be accepted, I will sign the lease provided within FIVE business days of being received. Should I fail to do so, the application shall be considered withdrawn. There will be no further obligation to reserve the rental, and my holding deposit will be forfeited.

6. I hereby waive any claim for damages if my application is not accepted.

7. I understand that every reasonable effort will be made to have the premises ready for occupancy as promised. However, should the premises not be available for occupancy on the date promised, I hereby waive all rights to seek to recover damages of any kind from the Landlord or Management Company.

8. I hereby authorize and permit the Landlord or Management Company to obtain any information necessary to verify the accuracy of any information or statements I have made on this application. I authorize and permit my credit report to be obtained and further authorize the Landlord or Management Company to make further credit inquiries regarding continued creditworthiness and for purposes of collection of unpaid rent or damages to premises, should that become necessary.

9. From time to time, I permit contact with my employer to verify my employment status during my tenancy.

10. I shall not hold the Owner or Management Company responsible for any allergic reactions to the premises, inside or outside, from me, other occupants, or guests. I shall check for allergic reactions before signing the Lease Agreement.

11. I certify that I am not manufacturing, using, storing, or selling dangerous controlled substances and understand that I will immediately be required to vacate the premises if evidence of such is found on the premises or if I am convicted of any crimes related to possession or distribution of controlled, dangerous substances.

12. I further understand and agree that the security deposit and rent must be paid in full by **money order** or **teller's check** before moving in. If I am unable to or fail for whatever reason to pay the balance of the amount due at that time, the application shall be considered withdrawn, and my holding deposit will be forfeited.

By: _____
(applicant's signature)   (applicant to print name)   (date)

By: _____
(applicant's signature)   (applicant to print name)   (date)

TENANT SCREENING - For The Small Asset Landlord

Employment Verification

To Whom It May Concern:

_____, has recently applied for housing from _____. To help in the selection process, please complete the following confidential questions, and fax this form back to us at your earliest convenience.

1.	**Employer's name and address.**			
2.	**Length of employment?**			
3.	**Job description?**			
4.	**Is the employee in good standing?**			
5.	**Employee hours?**			
6.	**Employee salary:**	Weekly $ _____	Monthly $ _____	Annually $ _____
	Commissions:	_____		

Employer's Signature:	
Telephone:	
Employee's authorization to release the above information.	
Employees Signature:	_____
Date:	_____

TENANT SCREENING - For The Small Asset Landlord

Landlord Verification

To Whom It May Concern:

_____, has recently applied for housing from _____. We ask you to assist us in this process, by completing the following confidential questions, and fax this form back to us at your earliest convenience.

1.	How long was the applicant your tenant?	
2.	What was the applicant's monthly rent?	
3.	Did the applicant pay their rent on time?	
4.	Were any complaints from tenants or neighbors ever registered against this applicant?	
5.	Did the applicant demonstrate respect for your apartment, its contents, and the surrounding property?	
6.	Would you recommend this applicant for tenancy?	
7.	How many people occupied this apartment?	

Landlord Name:

Telephone:

Landlord/Manager Signature: _____

Date: _____

Personal Guarantor

WHEREAS, _____ 'Lessee' has requested that _____ 'Landlord' enter into a Contract for the Lease of Real Estate for certain property located in the City of _____, County of _____, State of _____, more commonly known as _____, Apt. __, _____, _____.

WHEREAS, as an inducement to Landlord to enter into Contract for the Lease of Real Estate, _____ 'Guarantor' has agreed to personally guarantee the payment and performance of all of Lessee's obligations, conditions, and covenants as set forth in said Lease Agreement.

NOW, THEREFORE, FOR VALUABLE CONSIDERATION, the receipt and sufficiency of which is hereby acknowledged, Guarantor does hereby unconditionally guarantee that Lessee's obligations, conditions, and covenants will be performed strictly in accordance with the terms of said Lease Agreement regardless of any law, regulation, or order now or hereafter in effect in any jurisdiction affecting the rights of Landlord with respect thereto, to the same extent as if Guarantor under this Guaranty shall be absolute and unconditional irrespective of:

- A. Any lack of validity or enforceability of the Contract for the Lease Agreement.
- B. Any change in the time, manner, or place of payment of, or in any other term of, all or any of the obligations, or any other amendment or waiver of or any consent to departure from the Contract for the Lease Agreement.
- C. Any exchange, release, or non-perfection of any collateral, or any release or amendment or waiver of or consent to departure from any other guaranty, for all or any of the obligations.
- D. Any other circumstances that might otherwise constitute a defense available to, or a discharge of, the Lessee or any Guarantor.

This Guaranty is a continuing guaranty and shall (i) remain in full force and effect until the fulfillment of all of Lessee's obligations, conditions, and covenants under said Lease Agreement, (ii) be binding upon the Guarantor, its successors, and assigns, and (iii) inure to the benefit of and be enforceable by the Landlord and its respective successors, transferees, and assigns. Any liability of the Guarantor shall not be affected by, nor shall it be necessary to procure the consent of the Guarantor or give any notice in reference to, any settlement, or variation of terms of any obligation of the Lessee, or of a Guarantor or any other interested person, by operation of law or otherwise; nor by failure to file, record, or register any security document. Guarantor recognizes that Landlord may utilize various means of attempting to verify Lessee's compliance with the obligations and hereby expressly agrees that such steps are for the sole benefit of Landlord and the adequacy of performance of such checks and examinations shall not be considered as a defense to or mitigation of liability hereunder.

The Guarantor does hereby expressly waive and dispense with notice of acceptance of this Guaranty, notices of nonpayment or nonperformance, notice of amount of indebtedness outstanding at any time, protests, demands, and prosecution of collection, foreclosure, and possessory remedies. The undersigned hereby waives any right to require Landlord to (i) proceed against other persons or Lessee, (ii) advise Guarantor of the results of any checks or examinations, (iii) require Lessee to comply with its agreement with Landlord, or (iv) proceed against Lessee or proceed against or exhaust any security.

Except as noted, Landlord has made no promises to Lessee or Guarantor to induce execution of this Guaranty, and there are no agreements or understandings, either oral or in writing, between the parties affecting this Guaranty. The obligation of all parties signing this Guaranty, where more than one, shall be joint and several. No amendment or waiver of any provision of the Guaranty or consent to any departure by the Guarantor therefrom shall in any event be effective unless the same shall be in writing and signed by the Landlord.

This Guaranty may not be changed orally and shall bind and inure to the benefit of the heirs, administrators, successors, and assigns of the Lessee and Landlord, respectively. If any part of this Guaranty is not valid or enforceable according to applicable law, all other parts will remain enforceable. This Guaranty and the performance hereunder shall be construed and determined according to the laws of the State of _____.

IN WITNESS WHEREOF THE GUARANTOR HAS EXECUTED THIS GUARANTY this _____ day of _____, 20___

_____   _____
(guarantor)   (guarantor)

STATE OF   _____

COUNTY OF   _____

PERSONALLY, came and appeared before me, the undersigned in and for the jurisdiction aforesaid, the within named _____ and _____ in the above and foregoing instrument of writing, who acknowledged to me that they signed and delivered the above foregoing instrument of writing on the day and in the year and for the purposes therein mentioned.

     GIVEN under my hand and official seal of office on this the _____ day of _____, 20____

_____ NOTARY PUBLIC

MY COMMISSION EXPIRES: _____

House Rules and Policies

Sample

House Rules and Policies

> **Welcome to Your New Home!**
>
> Every effort will be made to provide you with a pleasant atmosphere in which to reside. To achieve this and ensure health, welfare, and safety, we ask all tenants to cooperate with the following House Rules and Policies, which are part of the Lease Agreement.
>
> **Your apartment is your home and should be treated in that respect.**
>
> **Please respect the property of others.**
>
> Repeated violations of these **House Rules and Policies** that disrupt the livability of the apartment community, adversely affect the health or safety of any person or the right of any Tenant to the quiet enjoyment of the leased premises or have any adverse effect on the management of the apartment community, will be deemed grounds for termination of the **Lease Agreement.**

House Rules and Policies

Section One

I. **GENERAL**
- This agreement is an addendum and part of the **Lease Agreement** between the **Landlord** and **Tenant**.
- New rules and policies or amendments to these rules may be adopted upon giving thirty (30) days' notice in writing. These rules and any changes or revisions have a legitimate purpose and are not intended to be arbitrary or work as a substantial modification of Tenant rights. They will not be unequally enforced. The tenant is responsible for the conduct of their guests and adherence to these rules and regulations at all times.
- The tenant cannot use the premises for anything unlawful or in such manner as to interfere unreasonably with the use by another occupant.
- Tenant shall not make any apartment-to-apartment canvass to solicit business or information or to distribute any article or material to or from other tenants or occupants of the community, and shall not exhibit, sell, or offer to sell, use, rent, or exchange any products or services in or from the apartment.
- When the Tenant has a new telephone number, they must communicate this information to the Landlord.

TENANT SCREENING - For The Small Asset Landlord

A. **NOISE AND CONDUCT**
   - Tenants shall not make or allow any disturbing noises in the apartment by tenant, family, or guests nor permit anything by such persons that will interfere with other persons' rights, comforts, or conveniences.
   - All musical instruments, television sets, stereos, radios, etc., are to be played at a volume that will not disturb other persons.
   - The activities and conduct of the tenant, tenant's guests, and minor children of tenant or guests outside of the apartment on the common grounds and parking areas must be reasonable at all times and not annoy or disturb other persons.
   - No lounging, visiting, or loud talking that may be disturbing to other tenants will be allowed in the common areas at any time.
   - No clothing, curtains, or other items shall be hung from balconies or out of windows.

B. **CLEANLINESS AND TRASH**
   - The apartment must be clean, sanitary, and free from objectionable odors.
   - The tenant shall assist management in keeping the common outside areas clean.
   - No littering of papers, cigarette butts, or trash is allowed.
   - No trash or other materials may be accumulated that will cause a hazard or violate any health, fire, or safety ordinance or regulation.
   - Garbage must be placed inside the containers provided, and lids should not be slammed. Garbage should not accumulate and should be placed in the outside containers daily.
   - Furniture must be kept inside the apartment. All personal belongings must be kept inside or in storage areas approved in writing by Management. Unless agreed to in writing, any items outside the apartment are subject to removal by Management. The tenant may be charged for the cost of removal.
   - Articles are not to be left in the hallways or common areas.
   - Clothing, curtains, rugs, etc., shall not be shaken or hung outside any ledge or balcony.

C. **SAFETY**
   - No smoking is allowed in the common areas of the property.
   - All doors must be locked during the absence of the tenant.
   - All appliances except refrigerators must be turned off before leaving the apartment.
   - When leaving for more than five (5) days, the Tenant shall notify management how long the Tenant will be away.
   - The use or storage of gasoline, cleaning solvent, or other combustibles in the apartment is prohibited.
   - No personal belongings, including bicycles, play equipment, or other items, may be placed in the halls, stairways, or about the building.
   - A responsible adult must supervise children on the premises at all times.
   - Candles may not be burned in bedrooms.

D. **MAINTENANCE, REPAIRS, AND ALTERATIONS**
   - The Tenant's responsibility shall include regularly testing the smoke and carbon monoxide detector(s) to ensure that the devices are in operable condition. In writing, the tenant will inform Management immediately of any defect, malfunction, or failure

of such detectors. The tenant is responsible for replacing batteries if needed unless otherwise prohibited by law.
- Tenant shall advise Management in writing of any items requiring repair (dripping faucets, faulty light switches, etc.). Notification should be immediate in an emergency or everyday problems within business hours. A repair request should be made as soon as the defect is noted.
- Service requests should not be made to maintenance people or other such personnel.
- Costs of repair or clearance of stoppages in waste pipes or drains, water pipes, or plumbing fixtures caused by Tenant's negligence or improper usage are the responsibility of Tenant. The Tenant must pay the payment for corrective action on demand.
- The tenant shall make no alterations or improvements without the consent of management. Any article attached to the woodwork, walls, floors, or ceilings shall be Tenant's sole responsibility. The tenant shall be liable for any repairs necessary during or after residency to restore premises to the original condition.

House Rules and Policies

Section Two

The following are general rules that you will be expected to follow:

ADVERTISEMENTS: Tenant shall not allow any sign, advertisement, or notice to be placed inside or outside the building. There will be **no** rummage or furniture sales. No signs, stickers, or notes are to be posted on the apartment entry door or windows.

ALCOHOL CONSUMPTION: Alcohol consumption is only allowed in the apartment or on your personal patio/porch area. Consumption of alcohol in any public/common area is not permitted.

ANTENNAS/DISHES: Tenant is not allowed to install a video antenna device or DBS satellite dish, hereinafter collectively referred to as a "dish."

APPLIANCES: The installation of a full-sized dishwasher, washing machine, and dryer is prohibited. With prior management approval, air conditioners (manufactured for the in-wall sleeves) are permitted.

BALCONIES AND PATIOS: All balconies and patios must be clean and neat. This includes but is not limited to no furnishings unless they are specifically designed for outdoor or lawn use, no beer kegs, no trash bins or cans, no storage of potentially dangerous, flammable, poisonous, or hazardous materials.

BANNED INDIVIDUALS FROM THE PROPERTY: Management reserves the right to ban any individual from the property and/or enter the building. Tenants are strictly forbidden to allow these individuals on the property or into the building. Tenants who allow banned individuals onto the property, into the building, or their units may be subject to eviction action as permitted by law.

CARPETING: The carpet installed in your apartment is flame resistant, as required by law. However, a burn hole will occur if hot ash is dropped on it. Burn holes or other damage to your carpet will be charged to the tenant. Please advise Management as soon as possible if any such incident should occur so that it may be corrected.

CARPET CLEANING DURING TENANCY: The tenant's responsibility is to keep the carpeting clean. Therefore, management recommends that Tenant have the carpeting professionally cleaned during their tenancy to avoid additional charges. **A filthy carpet is not considered normal wear and tear and is therefore subjected to an extra cleaning or replacement cost at move out.**

CARPET CLEANING AT MOVE-OUT: Tenant must have the carpet professionally cleaned at move out. A receipt must be presented by the last day of occupancy, or the tenant will be charged $100 per carpeted room for the cleaning. If the carpet is unable to be cleaned or needs to be replaced due to conditions made by the tenant, the tenant will be charged for the replacement of same, minus wear and tear.

CHARCOAL AND GAS GRILLS: Charcoal and gas grills are never to be used for any purpose within the apartment or on the patio or balcony of the apartment.

CEILINGS AND FLOORS: Tenants and their guests shall not damage or disturb any part of the ceiling or floor in the apartment in any way, including but not limited to installing hooks, nails, or other hardware in the ceiling; drilling in the ceiling; hanging plants, light fixtures, or other objects from the ceiling; allowing water to accumulate on the floor; and/or painting, repairing, or making improvements concerning the ceiling or floor. Tenant shall immediately report any sagging, warping, leaking, cracking, staining, holes, or water accumulation related to the ceiling or floor to Management. **Any damage the tenant causes to the ceiling or floor, including but not limited to damage caused by the tenant's violation of the above, shall not constitute ordinary wear and tear. The tenant shall be responsible for reimbursing Management for the cost of repairing damage to the ceiling or floor and any damages resulting from the tenant's action.**

CHRISTMAS TREE DISPOSAL: Once the holidays are over, please dispose of your tree as directed by Management.

CRIMINAL ACTIVITY: Criminal and drug activity committed by any household member is prohibited, whether on or off the property. Criminal and sex offender background checks will be run before the annual lease renewal process. Anyone who may be a threat to the health, safety, and welfare of other residents in the community will not have their lease renewed. Fair Housing laws do not protect criminal activity.

- Having a criminal record is not a protected class under fair housing laws.
- A **conviction** means that a judge and jury have determined that the individual is guilty of a particular crime. An **arrest** occurs if law enforcement suspects the individual committed a crime.

- **Adjudication withheld** means the court determined the individual did the crime, but the court is not entering a conviction at the moment. Instead, the court places certain conditions on the defendant (i.e., do community service; do not do drugs).

DAMAGE TO THE APARTMENT/COMMON AREAS: Tenants will be strictly held responsible for damages in their apartments and to the common areas. The tenant is also responsible for any damage done by their guests. A written bill will be sent shortly after the damage is noticed, and payment is expected promptly upon receipt. Further maintenance that is required beyond usual wear and tear will be charged to the tenant(s).

DELIVERIES/SOLICITATION: Management will not accept any deliveries for any tenants. No solicitation of any kind is permitted in the building or on the grounds.

DISTURBANCES: The tenant agrees not to permit noises, loud voices, acts, or odors that will disturb the rights or comfort of neighbors. The tenant agrees to keep the volume of any radio, CD player, stereo, television, or musical instrument at a level that will not disturb the neighbors. Tenants agree not to let their guests, visitors, or children disturb their neighbors as well.

ENTRANCES: No outside doors are to be propped open under any circumstances to allow tenants or visitors entry without using a key or the intercom system.

FIREARMS: Possession of weapons on the premises is **not** allowed under any circumstances.

FIRE EXTINGUISHERS: Every apartment has a five-pound ABC dry-chemical fire extinguisher.

FIRE EXTINGUISHER INSPECTIONS: In compliance with state and local fire codes, the fire extinguisher in your apartment must be inspected by a qualified outside agency once a year. This inspection requires entry into each apartment by inspection company personnel, accompanied by management. You will be given at least thirty days' notification.

FIREWORKS: Storing or using fireworks on the premises is strictly forbidden. This includes but is not limited to sparklers, Roman candles, bottle rockets, smoke bombs, firecrackers, etc.

GAMES: Skateboarding and games such as darts, baseball, softball, and stickball are not permitted on the property. Archery sets, B.B. guns, and anything that fires a projectile is considered a dangerous weapon and are **not allowed** on the property.

GARBAGE/RECYCLING: Tenant will not allow garbage, newspapers, or other refuse to remain in the apartment to litter the halls or the outside of the building. All garbage must be wrapped, tied, and deposited in the receptacles provided by Management.

GARAGE/CARPORT: The landlord grants permission to **tenants** to occupy the garage indicated in the Rent Summary on Page One (1) of this Lease Agreement. Tenant is subject to the following terms:

- The tenant acknowledges that the garage/carport is for the parking of vehicles only. The tenant acknowledges that the garages are not air-conditioned and that storing personal items in the garage is strictly prohibited. Therefore, the Landlord assumes no responsibility for personal belongings stored within the garage. Tenant shall not keep any pets in the garage nor store any explosives, fireworks, or any other item or substance that Landlord deems dangerous.

- No electricity may be hooked up to the garage or carport, and no plants may be grown within the garage or storage unit.
- Tenant further understands that the Landlord does not provide security services for Tenant or any of Tenant's belongings in the garage or carport. The landlord will not be liable for any damages, loss, or injury to persons or property occurring within or about the garage or carport, whether caused by the Landlord, someone else, weather, fire, rain, flood, or any other act of God.
- The tenant is responsible for the electronic door opener. The deposit, if placed, will be refunded if the door opener is returned upon move-out and is in operable condition.
- The tenant is responsible for the maintenance and care of the fixtures inside the garage and may not remove them for any reason.
- The tenant is responsible for all damages and agrees to reimburse the Landlord for all such damages.
- The garage door shall be closed at all times except for entering or exiting the garage.
- The landlord reserves the right to enter the garage for an inspection, repair, alteration, or other reasonable business purposes connected with the property's operation.

GASOLINE-POWERED EQUIPMENT: Gasoline, kerosene, solvents, and other flammable liquids are not to be stored in the building, apartment, hallways, or in storage areas.

GUESTS/VISITORS: Tenant shall be responsible for guests/visitors at all times. Guests/visitors are not allowed to loiter or play in the halls, stairways, elevators, lawns, or other areas used by the public and other tenants. Any person who stays longer than fourteen days in twelve months will be considered a tenant and violate the Lease Agreement provisions regarding household composition.

INSURANCE: The tenant must obtain their own personal renter's insurance. The Owner and Management are not responsible for theft or the damage to personal property from any source in the apartments, laundry room, storage area, or any other portions of the premises. A copy of the policy must be given to Landlord.

KEYS: Each tenant will receive two (2) apartment door keys, two (2) apartment deadbolt keys, two (2) vestibule door keys, and one (1) mailbox key. If the keys are lost or stolen, there will be a replacement charge to the tenant: apartment door key: $10.00; apartment deadbolt key: $15.50; vestibule door key: $7.00; mailbox key: $15.00; key fobs: $50.00 when used. Chain locks are not permitted.

LAUNDRY ROOM: Washers and dryers are for the use of the tenants. The washing and drying of laundry by outsiders are prohibited. Each tenant is responsible for leaving the laundry room neat and orderly and following all instructions for equipment use. Note: Lint must be removed from the dryer with each use for efficiency and fire safety. Lint should be placed in the appropriate garbage containers. No one is allowed to leave their laundry in the washer or dryer for thirty minutes after completion without it being removed to a basket or a folding table to let someone else use the washer and dryer. If a machine is not functioning correctly, place the out-of-order sign on it and call the appropriate service number. Management will not be liable for any loss, damage, or injury to persons or property from whatever cause due to the Tenant's use of the laundry equipment.

LIGHTS: The tenant is responsible for replacing lightbulbs within their apartment.

LIVE-IN AIDE: There are times that a tenant may require a **live-in aide** to live with them due to a disability. If the tenant requests that the aide not be on the lease or the income-certification paperwork, this situation will be determined by the following assessment:

- Is there enough physical room to house the aide?
- Will having the aide impose an undue hardship, including an unreasonable financial burden?
- Will the aide hold up to a background check?

LOCKS: Tenant shall not attach or permit additional locks or similar devices to any door or window, change existing locks or the mechanism thereof, or make or permit to be made any keys for any entrance other than those provided by Management. Upon the termination of tenancy, the Tenant shall deliver to the manager all keys that have been furnished Tenant or that Tenant has made, and in the event of loss of any keys, to pay Management for replacement.

LOITERING: Loitering is not permitted on the lawns, sidewalks, entries, halls, stairways, or parking areas.

MOVE-OUT PRIOR TO THE EXPIRATION OF LEASE: Each tenant must realize that moving out prior to the expiration of the lease does not release either the individual or other tenants (and guarantors if applicable) on the lease. All tenants are jointly and severally liable for the full performance of all lease obligations. This means you are each responsible for your roommates. Management does not differentiate between you individually; you are all treated as a group with respect to this. If you move out before the expiration of the lease, you must notify Management in writing and return your keys. You will remain responsible for payment of rent and other charges until the earlier of the original expiration of your lease or our leasing the apartment to new tenants who take possession. In addition, you may be held responsible for leasing costs that may include but are not limited to cleaning the apartment, painting, advertising, etc. If you move out and fail to pay rent, Management may go to court and obtain a judgment for monetary damages against all or one of the tenants and one or all of the guarantors of the lease. If an individual moves out of the apartment and the others remain, all those on the lease will be bound by the lease terms. However, should you want to assign part of the lease to a new individual, you must come to the office and have a release signed by all tenants on the current lease and a new lease signed (including an approved application with complete papers from the new tenant).

OBSTRUCTIONS: The sidewalks, entries, halls, and stairways will not be blocked or used for any purposes other than entering or exiting the respective apartments. No recreational equipment or personal items will be permitted or kept in the hallways or stairways.

PETS: Tenant(s) are/are not permitted to keep cats or dogs (except assistance dogs) in the apartment or on the premises. Any animal found on the premises is subject to immediate removal by Management. Animals will not be returned to the tenant or neighbor but the town's animal shelter. If we become aware for any reason of an animal living in an apartment, the tenants shall receive a written notice immediately that they have five (5) days to remove the animal, or eviction proceedings will commence.

PET GUIDELINES: Only one (1) of the following types is permitted per apartment:

- Birds
    - maximum number: two (2)
    - must be maintained **inside** the cage at all times
    - no larger than a cockatoo
- Fish and turtles
    - maximum aquarium size: twenty (20) gallons
    - must be maintained properly and on an approved stand
    - turtles must be inside the aquarium

NO OTHER TYPES OF PETS MAY BE KEPT IN THE APARTMENT.

RECEIVE YOUR FULL DEPOSIT BACK WHEN YOU MOVE: This list is provided as part of your **Lease Agreement** to be aware of property damage costs and avoid these expenses by doing what is necessary to get your deposit back.

Cleaning (not done by you)	Bathroom cabinets and floor	$25
	Bathtub/shower and surrounding area	$30
	Carpet cleaning or deodorizing	$150–$250
	Extensive cleaning	$90
	Fireplace	$125
	Kitchen cabinet or countertop	$45
	Kitchen or bathroom floor	$50
	Oven	$30–$100
	Refrigerator	$70–$150
	Stove hood	$30
	Stovetop or oven	$30–$100
	Toilet and sink	$20
	Windows (each)	$90 per hour
Damages	Remove crayon marks	$75
	Minor/extensive nail hole repair	$55
	Patch sheetrock, compound, and sand	$50–$200
	Replace interior/exterior door	$175–$400
	Replace sliding glass door	$775
	Replace faucets	$195
	Replace bathroom mirror or cabinets	$90–$175
	Replace showerheads	$75
	Replace toilet	$350
	Replace garbage disposal	$275
	Replace countertop	$250–$450
	Repair windowpane	$75–$225
	Replace blinds	$85
	Replace tile/linoleum	$300–$500
Missing items	Replace lightbulb	$3
	Light fixture globe	$20
	Electrical outlet/switch	$15
	Electrical cover plate	$5
	Replace key	$5
	Replace shower curtain	$25
	Replace refrigerator shelf	$35
	Replace oven knob	$16

TENANT SCREENING - For The Small Asset Landlord

GENERAL REPAIRS	
Replace refrigerator shelf	$35
Replace stove/oven knob	$16
Repair ceramic tile	$150
Replace countertop	$275
Replace cutting board	$40
Replace kit/bath cabinet knobs	$10
Replace mirror	$45
Replace medicine cabinet	$100
Replace towel bar	$22
Replace tub/shower enclosure	$195
Regrout bath/shower tiles	$165
Repair porcelain	$135
Replace thermostat	$75
Replace fire extinguisher	$55
Remove junk and debris	$250
Replace doorbell button	$15
Replace doorbell unit	$50

PLUMBING	
Replace kitchen faucet	$195
Replace bathroom faucet	$195
Replace shower head	$75
Replace the toilet tank lid	$45
Replace toilet seat	$35
Replace toilet	$350
Replace garbage disposer	$275
Snake toilet	$45
Clear sewer/cesspool line	$95

ELECTRICAL	
Replace lightbulb	$3
Replace light fixture globe	$20
Replace light fixture	$55
Replace electrical outlet/switch	$15
Replace the electrical cover plate	$5

FLOORING	
Remove carpet stains	$80
Cigarette burn in carpet/floor	$80
Deodorize carpet	$80
Repair carpet	$150
Repair hardwood floor	$95
Refinish hardwood floor	$380
Repair linoleum	$85
Replace bathroom linoleum	$385
Replace kitchen linoleum	$385
Replace floor tile	$75
Replace ceramic tile	$150

WALLS	
Remove mildew and treat the surface	$75
Cover crayon/marker/pen marks	$75
Repair hole in the wall	$55
Remove wallpaper	$175
Repaint (per wall/ceiling)	$55

DOORS	
Repair hole in the hollow-core door	$55
Repair forced door damage	$75
Replace door (inside)	$175
Replace door (outside)	$400
Replace sliding glass door	$775
Replace sliding door screen	$65

WINDOWS & TREATMENT	
Replace windowpane	$225
Replace venetian or mini-blind	$85
Replace window shade	$15
Replace window screen	$25
Replace vertical blinds (sliding door)	$175

LOCKS	
Replace key	$5
Replace door lock	$47
Replace interior doorknob	$28
Replace deadbolt lock	$47

GROUNDS/EXTERIOR	
Major yard cleanup	$425
Minor yard cleanup	$225
Mow lawn front and back	$50
Clean gutters	$185
Trim bushes	$35

EXTERMINATING	
Exterminate for cockroaches	$550
Exterminate for fleas	$375

REPAIRS/MAINTENANCE: If you have items in your apartment that need repair, call the office at XXX-XXX-XXXX Monday through Friday between 8:00 a.m. and 4:30 p.m. Please do not wait until a repair becomes an **emergency repair**. **We provide EMERGENCY SERVICE during the hours of 4:30 p.m. and 8:00 a.m., Monday through Friday.** *If on-call staff is called out to your apartment at your request and it is not an emergency, you will be charged for the actual staff time.*

- The tenant agrees to pay for all necessary repairs costing less than $300.
- There is no charge for repairing items in the apartment generated by normal wear and tear or component failure.
- Repair of damages or failures caused by the tenant, family member, or a tenant guest will be paid by the tenant.
- Unless of an emergency nature, no maintenance work will be performed on Saturdays, Sundays, or legal holidays. The only requests considered an emergency are those that endanger life, health, or property, not an inconvenience.

ROOF ACCESS: Admittance to the roof of the building is restricted to maintenance personnel and antennae licenses and is not otherwise permitted.

SEX OFFENDERS REGISTRY: Management does its best to protect the community against **sex offenders** during the application period. The tenant's responsibility is to check the Internet and see who may move into the neighborhood.

- Family Watch Dog - http://www.familywatchdog.us/
- FBI Sex Offender Registry - http://www.fbi.gov/scams-and-safety/sex-offender-registry

SMOKE DETECTOR: Smoke detectors are located in each apartment. Smoke detectors will be checked twice during regular semiannual apartment inspections. It is a violation of state and local laws to disable the smoke detector in any manner or to cover the sensor with any material.

SMOKING: Smoking is prohibited in all public areas of the building, including lobbies.

STINK BUGS: Management will contract with a **professional pest exterminator** to determine whether there is a problem and what course of action to take to eliminate the problem.

Management will pay the cost of the extermination contractor and the treatment of the apartment. In addition to the exterminator, the tenant must allow Management to have a contractor caulk all openings to the outside and repair all damaged screens and doors.

TENANT FEEDBACK FORM: The property owner wants to provide you with the best level of service possible. To achieve that goal, your feedback on what Management does well and areas that can be improved is most important. Please return the questionnaire as soon as possible after receipt.

TENANT-BILLED SERVICES: Tenant will be billed by Management for additional rent, fees, and charges for all other services requested that are beyond the scope of the **Lease Agreement**. Payment is expected promptly after receipt.

USE OF PREMISES: Tenant shall occupy and use the premises as a private residence and for no other purpose. Tenant shall not carry on any trade, profession, business, school course of instruction, or entertainment on the premises.

UTILITIES/CABLE: Tenant is responsible for contacting utility/cable companies to transfer services into their name.

UTILITY WASTEAGE: Tenant shall not waste electricity, water, heat, air conditioning, or other utilities or services, and agrees to cooperate fully with Management to assure the most effective and energy-efficient operation of the building and shall not allow the adjustment of any controls. As a condition to claiming any deficiency in the air conditioning or ventilation services provided by Management, the tenant shall close any blinds or drapes in the apartment to prevent or minimize direct sunlight.

WINDOWS: Tenant shall not cover or obstruct any window or door. All window coverings shall have a white or off-white fire-resistant back.

If any provision of these **House Rules and Policies** is or should become prohibited under any law, that provision shall be made ineffective without invalidating any remaining provisions.

The undersigned Tenant(s) acknowledge(s) having read and understands the foregoing and receipt of a duplicate original.

_____ _____ _____ _____

Tenant   Date   Tenant   Date

_____ _____ _____ _____

Tenant   Date   Tenant   Date

Letter of Acceptance

date

name

street

city, state, zip

This letter confirms our conversation on [date] at [time], in which you accepted our offer to rent the apartment at [rental property address]. As we discussed, these are the rental terms:

Rent $ Deposit $

Rental start date: 20_____

Rental term: One-year lease, ending on 20_____

Number of occupants: _____

NO PETS

Deposit and first month's rent total $_____ to be paid by cashier's check or money order on or before _____ 20_____ at this address: [landlord's address].

Holding deposit of ___[amount] $___ to be paid by ___[date]___ at this address _____. We will sign the rental documents on ___[date]___ at ___[time]___ at ___[address]___.

Thank you for deciding to live here. I look forward to working with you to ensure that your move-in and tenancy are smooth and enjoyable. If you have any questions, please do not hesitate to call me.

Yours truly,

_____

Landlord (Property Owner)

Acceptance Letter with Lease Agreement

Date:

Re:

Dear

Thank you for considering making [rental address] your new home. The information you have provided on your application has been verified, and we would like to take this opportunity to welcome you.

The Lease Agreement has been prepared, and we are enclosing it for your review. Please return both copies with your signature so that we can complete the processing of your new apartment home.

Remember that time is of the essence with your paperwork.

Sincerely,

Landlord (Property Owner)

(Note: This letter and the Lease Agreement should be sent out certified mail, return receipt requested.)

Welcome New Resident

We hope that you will enjoy your new home. To assist you in getting settled, we would like to take this opportunity to explain some of our services and the property's policies, procedures, and rules.

MANAGEMENT

Managements maintains the following schedule:

Monday through Friday	10:00 a.m. to 4:00 p.m.
Saturday	10:00 a.m. to 2:00 p.m.
Sunday	CLOSED

If you have any problem or need any information about your residence, please feel free to call us at (XXX) XXX-XXX

PAYMENT OF RENT

Rents are due in full on the first of the month. Make checks payable to:

_____

Mail checks to: _____

Your rent becomes delinquent on the tenth day of the month. Payments not received by the tenth of the month are subject to a $100 late charge (and an additional $2 for each subsequent day until the delinquent rent is paid). You may also make a cash payment to the landlord to stop additional penalties.

MAINTENANCE

You are responsible for the routine upkeep of your residence. You are responsible for making all necessary repairs costing less than $300. Please contact the Resident Manager during regular working hours to request service. If an emergency occurs when the office is closed, please call: (XXX) XXX-XXX

Management is responsible for maintenance and repairs necessitated by normal wear and usage. Repair of damage caused by resident negligence or misuse is the resident's responsibility. In such cases, the maintenance staff will make the repairs, but the resident will be charged for the cost of labor and materials.

TENANT SCREENING - For The Small Asset Landlord

Reason for Non-Acceptance

Date:

Re: Reason for Non-acceptance

Dear Applicant,
Your request for tenancy has been denied for a reason indicated below:

	Application incomplete		Unable to verify employment
	Insufficient credit references		Temporary or irregular employment
	Unable to verify credit references		Length of employment
	No credit file		Insufficient income
	Delinquent credit obligations		Bankruptcy
	Profit and loss account(s)		Previous eviction(s)
	Excessive obligations		Garnishment, foreclosure, or repossession
	We do not offer rentals on the terms you have requested.		Because of negative information received from a second party
	Charge-offs		Too short a period of residence
	Insufficient personal references		Other
	A more qualified applicant for the rental		
	Information contained in a consumer credit report obtained from one or more agencies. (See list below.)			
	A consumer credit report containing insufficient information to meet our requirements was obtained from (see the list below):			
	Information was received from a person or company other than a consumer reporting agency. Under Section 615(b) of the Fair Credit Reporting Act, you have a right to make a written request to us within sixty days of receiving this letter for a disclosure of the nature of this information.			
	Because our decision was based on information in your credit history, Section 615(a) of the Fair Credit Reporting Act requires that we provide you with the source of that report. A checkmark indicates each agency that provided information about your credit history. The agency took no part in deciding to reject your application and cannot explain why the decision was made.			

	Equifax https://www.equifax.com 1-888-548-7878
	Experian https://www.experian.com/ 1-800-493-1058
	TransUnion https://www.transunion.com/ 1-800-916-8800

You have certain rights under federal law regarding your credit history. During the sixty-day period that starts _____, you have the right to receive a free copy of your consumer report from any consumer reporting agency whose name is checked above.

You have a right to dispute the accuracy or completeness of any information contained in your credit report, as furnished by the reporting agency whose name is checked above. If you believe your file contains errors or is inaccurate or incomplete, call the consumer reporting agency at its toll-free number listed above, or write to the address listed.

You have a right to put into your file a consumer statement up to one hundred words in length to explain items in your file. Trained personnel are available to help you with the consumer statement.

You may have additional rights under your state's credit reporting or consumer protection laws. Contact your local consumer protection agency or a state attorney general's office.

Sincerely

AFTERWORD

Thank you for reading

TENANT SCREENING
For the Small Asset Landlord

We hope you enjoyed this Real Estate Knowledge Publication

Thank you again, valued reader,
and we hope to meet you again on another book.

ABOUT THE AUTHOR

Pierre Mouchette is the Founder and CEO of Real Property Experts LLC. He is a graduate of New York University, with a Master's in Business Administration, a Certificate in Real Estate Law - Fairfield University - C.T., a Graduate of the Realtors Institute - C.T., and held licensing as a Real Estate Broker, and a Mortgage Broker.

Pierre is currently authoring Books, Booklets, How-to-Articles, and Guides in retirement. Pierre has an extensive background in real estate investment, business management, and sales, supplemented by decades of hands-on experience in building systems engineering, development, evaluation, and various analytical engineering studies.

Pierre launched Real Property Experts in 2013 to simplify real estate investing by connecting investors through innovative technology using background knowledge and experience. In 2018, Pierre created THE SYNCHRONICITY INVESTOR, a real estate website to facilitate world-class solutions for real estate investors and investment businesses.

	REAL PROPERTY EXPERTS LLC
	- presents -
	Real Estate Knowledge Publications

RESIDENTIAL SMALL ASSET INVESTOR	**HOW TO**	
		How To Stat and Propagate Your Real Estate Farm
		How To Be A Real Estate Investor
	INVESTMENT	
		Raising The Family Without Taking A Hit
		TENANT MANAGEMENT - For The Small Asset Landlord
		TENANT SCREENING - For The Small Asset Landlord
		The Art Of Being "The Landlord"
		The Multifamily Buyer's Manual or The Art of Purchasing Your Multifamily Home Investment
		The Resident Manager's Handbook

www.ingramcontent.com/pod-product-compliance
Lightning Source LLC
Chambersburg PA
CBHW082118220526
45472CB00009B/2226